A Sure Foundation

Stability Through Life's Storms

Annette E. Williams

STRENGTH IN CHRIST
PUBLICATIONS

A Sure Foundation
by Annette Williams
Copyright © 2014

International Standard Book Number: 978-0-9907963-0-5

Cover Design: Samantha Malinay

Scripture quotations are from *The Holy Bible: Authorized King James Version*

Printed in the United States of America

Endorsements

"What a pleasure and great honor it was to be given the opportunity to preview the content of this book by Annette Williams. Pastoral joy is sometimes measured in the lives of the people we shepherd and Annette and her husband, Stephen, fueled that joy for my wife, Shirley, and me while they were part of our church community. This book is written from the perspective of extensive Kingdom experience but it flows from a woman of God's heart that desires to positively impact the lives of others. Thanks, Annette, for this insightful work that honors the validity of Biblical principles and highlights the importance of being led by the Spirit! I enjoyed the experience!"

Pastor Michael Mullins
Senior Pastor, Triumph Centre
Albuquerque, New Mexico
www.triumphabq.org

ക്കക്കക്കക്കക്കക്കക്കക്കക്കക്കക്കക്ക

"The bible tells us that our steps are ordered of the Lord. (Psalms 37:23) Fourteen years ago that is exactly what happened to me when the Promise Keepers Men's Ministry asked me to fill in during the August, 2000, New Mexico conference for one of the speakers who was called away with a family issue.

As a national Promise Keeper's speaker we are asked to give our availability for the conference season earlier in the year and this event in New Mexico fell on a bad weekend for me. My schedule had to be rearranged to meet this obligation.

The event was full with over 10 thousand men in attendance and one of these men, serving as a volunteer, was J. Stephen Williams. His wife Annette Williams, the author of this wonderful book, was also there as a volunteer helping with the registration and accounting department. I didn't know them and neither did they know me. They had no expectation to see me since I was just there as a fill in and not scheduled on the original program.

Four years later at my church in Charlotte, NC a gentleman came up to me and asked if I spoke in New Mexico at the Promise Keepers' meeting. He told me he was there and had now moved to Charlotte. He was impressed by my message and sought me out while he and Annette were looking for a new church home. Needless to say they found that church home with us and Stephen is now one of my Elders and Annette works as my Executive Assistant.

One of the things that has blessed me about working with Annette is the fact that the things mentioned in this book that she has faced didn't turn her a shade of bitter. If she didn't tell you about them you would never know she went through them. She is always full of joy and is willing to help people any way she can.

Therefore this isn't a book with a foundation of theory but a foundation of experience. I know you have heard, "Experience is the best teacher." But I like to say, "Someone else's experience is the best teacher!" Why should I go through what someone else has already proven through their experience doesn't work? And why shouldn't I try what has already been proven to work?

This is book is full of hope for people who have lost hope because Annette found the center of hope in Jesus Christ. I *recommend you read this book and then purchase a second one to loan or give to the people who need to believe again.*

Thanks Annette for writing this insightful and inspiring work and may God bless you and this book!"

Bishop Larry Jackson
Senior Pastor, Bethel Outreach International Church
Charlotte, North Carolina

Author's note: For ministry resources by Bishop Larry Jackson; books, CDs, DVDs, and more please visit www.betheloic.com and www.truevalueofawoman.com. His teachings will strongly impact your life for Christ and stretch you beyond what you could ever imagine.

Dedication

This book is first and foremost dedicated to Elder Stephen Williams, the other part of me, we are truly one and I am so very grateful to you for choosing me and leading our union as we live for God. Thank you for being the living example of Christ in my life.

Secondly, I dedicate and thank the people of God who taught me through the years including my uncle and first pastor, the late Reverend Clifton Jones, and most notably the pastors that I had the privilege to serve with as I traveled during my Air Force career and beyond; Pastor Alexander who introduced me to the gifting of the Holy Spirit; Pastor Walter Brown who opened my eyes to the occult world and showed me a biblical world view; Pastor Phil Privette who performed my wedding ceremony to Stephen; Pastor Steve Brown, a faithful and true friend; Bishop Courtney McBath; a caring leader who taught us spiritual freedom; Pastor, Dr. Michael D. Sproul, who helped me overcome the pain of infertility; Pastor Michael Mullins, who gave me a living example of love and caring; Apostle Raymond Luster who tirelessly taught me how to defend what I believe; and my current pastor, mentor and big brother, Bishop Larry Jackson who has stretched me, guided me, and given me a deeper and more meaningful understanding of the word of God. These faithful men of God have helped me throughout my Christian walk and I am forever grateful to each one of them.

I also dedicate this book to the multitude of family and friends, with special acknowledgment to my sister, Zelda Moore, who have been with me and helped me navigate through life enabling me to build a strong and *A Sure Foundation*.

Forward

I've been told that you learn by one of two ways - by revelation or tribulation. A child either listens to the warning of her parent or is found crying from pain to learn that a hot stove is not something you should touch with your bare hands. Unfortunately I've learned many important things about God's law and character by tribulation. For the things I was able to learn through revelation I am very grateful to those that I've learned from; those who were transparent enough to share their experiences with me so that I would not go through a similar misfortune.

It is with this in mind that I wrote this book and included personal experiences that will hopefully inspire and teach you. Jesus has given us clear instruction on how to remain steadfast but often we need encouragement from the testimony of another to help us better understand. I praise God for this great opportunity to serve.

As you read this book I pray you are inspired to study the word of God more deeply and spend more time developing a relationship with the only One who can keep you and help you stand firmly in this unstable and rocky world.

Blessings to you!

That I may publish with the voice of thanksgiving, and tell of all thy wondrous works. Psalm 26:7

ঌTable of Contentsঌ

Introduction

Every physical building needs a proper foundation to keep it from falling over or toppling to the ground during winds storms, earthquakes, or any type of inclement weather. These events are inevitable and must be prepared for. Our lives also should be formulated with a proper foundation so that life's "inclement weather"- money problems, sickness, and even the death of a loved one won't topple us to the ground.

This book came about by me asking the question, "What does God require of me?" I believe He led me to read the words of Jesus, the words in red in a red letter Bible. The words that I focused on were Matthew 5:3 through 7:27. These words of Jesus are words that He spoke to the multitudes during His sermon on the mount. Through this teaching He outlines how we should live our lives individually, toward others and toward God. If we apply these instructions to our lives we will have the sure foundation as described in Matthew; my house, my life, my eternal existence will be built on a rock, a sure foundation.

> *Therefore whosoever heareth these sayings of mine, and doeth them, I will liken him unto a wise man, which built his house upon a rock: And the rain descended, and the floods came, and the winds blew, and beat upon that house; and it fell not: for it was founded upon a rock.* Matthew 7: 24-25

And we will be perfect, complete in various applications of labor, growth, mental and moral character. Matthew 5:48

This book will give you a materials listing of what you need for your foundation. Most foundations are built using concrete, stone or cinder blocks. Each section in this book is depicted as a cinder block that you will need to build the foundation for your life; an individual cinder block, a response toward others cinder block, and a response toward God cinder block. As you read though this book imagine your life as a building and discover how it is indeed possible to build a strong, sure foundation for life.

Please note that before you build your foundation, just as you would need if you were building an actual physical structure, you must have the proper location. The proper location for your life's building is a repented heart towards God; being born again. If you have not repented and received the completed works of Jesus Christ making Him your personal Lord and Savior won't you take the time to do so now? Read the following prayer and accept Jesus into your life.

Dear Jesus, I acknowledge that I am a sinner and have fallen short of what You require of me. I have lived my life for myself and done things that please only me. I am sorry for this Lord and I repent and I ask you to forgive me. I believe with my heart and I confess with my mouth that You were born of a virgin, crucified on the cross for me and resurrected from the dead. I am saved. I come to you now and ask you to take control of my life; I give it fully to you. Help me to live every day in a way that pleases you. It is in Your name I pray. Amen.

By saying this prayer from a sincere heart you have entered into the Kingdom of Heaven. Seek out a Bible believing church that can nurture your new status as a citizen of heaven and help you grow as a mature Christian.

Once you have the proper location, a born again life; you can begin to learn how to build a sure foundation.

ONE

A Sure Foundation Defined

Properly-built buildings start with a foundation that will carry the weight of the building and prevent it from tumbling down from the natural forces around it.

The following is a brief outline on building foundations. It will help you understand why it is important to ensure your foundation is sure.

Survey and Stake

Before any construction can begin, the home site is surveyed to establish the home's basic footprint and to ensure the home is set back the appropriate distances from the property lines. The corners of the home are marked by surveyor's stakes. Offset stakes, which are about two feet out from the surveyor's stakes, also are placed. The excavator will dig at the offset stakes, creating a slightly larger hole than the foundation actually will occupy. The extra room enables crews to work on the exterior of the foundation walls.

Excavation

The depth of the excavation is determined by a structural engineer who considers the soil, the frost line and the height of the water table (the depth in the soil at which you find water). Surface soil is removed to expose soil that is compacted enough to bear the load of the home. The excavation must be deep enough to place the top of the footing below the frost line. This prevents the concrete from cracking due to the freeze-thaw cycle of the surrounding soil. The excavation cannot be so deep that it's below the water table, however, because that can cause a chronically wet or flooded basement.

Footings
Footings are poured concrete pathways that help to spread the weight of the home from the foundation walls to the surrounding soil. Footings are wider than the foundation walls they support, and form the perimeter of the home. Sometimes, additional footings are added inside the perimeter to support load-bearing interior walls.

Walls
Foundation walls are constructed by pouring concrete between sets of form work (the total system of support assemblies for freshly poured concrete, including mold, hardware and necessary bracing.) Once the concrete gains its full strength, the form work is removed. Foundation wall thickness is determined by a structural engineer who considers the height of the wall and the load it has to bear. (Structural load is the force or combination of forces of gravity, wind, and earth that acts upon the

structural system of a home). Wall thickness varies from home to home, and even within a home.[1]

A properly-built foundation will enable a building to stand up against the forces around it. I experienced the benefits of a properly-built foundation and know full well the importance of having one. As a Non-commissioned Officer in the United States Air Force I was sent on assignment to Andersen AFB, Guam. My husband and I arrived and were placed in temporary housing while we waited for our permanent housing to become available. The temporary housing was a two-story concrete building with the look of an institution rather than a comfortable home. I was a little discouraged to be living in such an ugly place but we made the best of it. I used wrapping paper to cover an unsightly hole in the wall and put decorative touches around the room to make it comfortable. Little did I know that this ugly concrete building would save me and my husband from injury and possible death.

After only 3 weeks in our concrete abode at 6:34 P.M. local time on Sunday, August 8, 1993, an 8.2 magnitude earthquake hit the little island of Guam. I had experienced earthquakes before when visiting California but nothing anywhere near this magnitude. My husband and I had just arrived back at the temporary lodging after celebrating our 5th wedding anniversary in an island hotel that weekend

---

[1] http://www.diynetwork.com/remodeling/basic-steps-of-building-a-foundation/index.html, March 11, 2014

and initially thought a very low flying aircraft was passing overhead. We soon realized this was no aircraft. The noise increasingly got louder and sounded more like a large freight train. Everything around us began to shake and we were immobilized by the enormity of the moment. We grabbed hands and prayed while the earth continued to shake violently. We thought the building would come crashing down but instead of crashing the building felt like rubber as it undulated and rolled with the moving earth beneath it. When things calmed down we went outside to see if anyone was hurt or if conditions were unsafe and we were astonished to see that everyone around us was fine and the damage to the building was minor.

The building was built with reinforced concrete mostly to withstand the frequent typhoons that raged across the small island but to the surprise of many they also withstood the effects of that earthquake. This same foundational structure was the norm throughout the Air Force base and many places on the island. Some structures across the island that were not as structurally sound did incur severe damage but thankfully very little human injury and no fatalities occurred.

The architects and builders on the island of Guam were wise enough to build foundations that hold up during very violent storms. They knew they would need to plan for the wind storms but the precautions they took inadvertently also protected the buildings against the unexpected earthquake. If we build the proper foundation for our lives we can also withstand the storms that come; those that are more common that most people face like temporary financial shortfalls or minor accidents but the proper foundation will also help us withstand the unexpected calamities such as the ones I've had to face; losing both parents as a child, divorce, homelessness and the inability to have children. Individually each of these events are devastating but being able to withstand all them without completely falling down takes a sure foundation.

In the Bible, Matthew 7:25 Jesus explains to us the story of the wise man who built his house on a rock; *"[25]and the rain descended, and the floods came, and the winds blew and beat upon that house; and it fell not, for it was founded upon a rock."* Jesus is speaking about Himself as the foundation rock. He clearly explains in the first part of verse 24 how to build on the rock; *"Therefore whosoever heareth these sayings of mine, and doeth them, I will liken him unto a wise man, which built his house upon a rock..."*
The portion of sayings that Jesus spoke, included in this book, are contained in Matthew 5:3 through 7:27. These words of Jesus are words that He spoke to the multitudes during His historical Sermon on the Mount. He also tells us in the book of John that if we don't keep His sayings we don't love Him.

He that loveth me not keepeth not my sayings: and the word which ye hear is not mine, but the Father's which sent me. John 14:24

Many commentaries and studies have been done on the passages of scripture found in the Sermon on the Mount. I don't claim to have the deep theological knowledge of what they mean but what I do have is a personal experience of what I believe Jesus is telling us and hope to outline it in a way that will help you understand, like I have, how to build a foundation that will withstand life's storms.

To start building the foundation as we saw above we need to survey and stake the location and begin excavation. This I compare with developing the foundation for our individual self which I believe is where Jesus' teaching begins. The next two chapters will expand on this theory.

❧TWO❧

The Need for God - Survey and Stake

Why You Shouldn't Do it Alone

Jesus' Sermon on the Mount in Matthew chapter 5 begins with the statement: "Blessed are the poor in spirit: for theirs is the kingdom of heaven." To be poor in spirit is to humble yourself and get rid of the pride of thinking you can handle your life on your own.

Think about it this way; God created me, so why wouldn't I put my total trust and faith in my creator? The creator knows the exact reason for which He made you and your intended purpose. He knows every inch of His creation and what it can and cannot withstand. Without the help from the creator you are guessing and speculating on how to live life.

Going back to the building analogy, if you fail to consult the architect and the blueprints for the building to find out the purpose and design, you will be guessing on the dimensions and reason for which the building is even being built. The architect for our lives is God and the blueprint is the Bible.

Set Boundaries

When staking out your property location, four stakes are placed to designate the boundary of the building. We must also set boundaries in our lives to make sure the building is built correctly. Without proper boundaries the building may be lopsided and very unstable. When we set boundaries based on the word of God we can be assured that our building will be solid and not easily toppled.

God's laws are the boundaries we should set and personal boundaries should be set based on the principle of God's word. I have certain boundaries against things in my life that are not necessarily illegal or sinful but if left unchecked could violate a principle that God has set.

For example, my husband and I are proponents of stewardship and believe everything God gives us should be properly cared for. We live by a budget and handle our finances in the way we believe pleases God. Therefore one of my personal boundaries is to donate an item of clothing whenever I purchase a similar item. If I buy a blouse, I find a blouse to donate from my closet.

This action does two things; one, it keeps me from impulse spending on clothing because I am constantly aware that I will have to get rid of something and, two it keeps my closet from becoming overstuffed.

It's important to keep God's law but it is also important to set personal boundaries that keep you on track with the principles of God.

Letting Go

It's also necessary to dig out your soil and make it bigger so the crew will have room to work and I liken this to letting go of your own thoughts and desires and giving God the room to work on you and fill you with His thoughts and desires.

You should never try to live your life based on how you feel or what you think because your mind and soul are not reliable sources of information. When I was growing up I loved the Cinderella story and based my views of love and marriage on it. I believed I would be rescued by a man and live happily ever after. Don't laugh, there are many young women that have this fantasy based on the media and have never been taught what love and marriage really is about.

Because of my beliefs I entered a marriage for all the wrong reasons and thought because I was married my life would be great. I totally ignored the abusive and failed marriages of family members. I never asked questions nor did I seek help from anyone. Most importantly I did not seek help from my creator, nor did I consult the Bible. I just knew in my own head that everything would be just like I wanted it to be. I was ignorant and naive and did not have a proper foundation.

After a few years of unhappiness I finally turned to the God of my childhood, the One to Whom I confessed the sinner's prayer from my heart to at age 11, and asked Him for help. I rededicated my life to Him and began to read the blueprint He left for us; the Bible. My life did not immediately change; I went through a separation that culminated in a reconciliation and renewal of marriage vows. After spending 8 years enlisted in the US Air Force I ended my career and chose to join the man to whom I was married on his assignment to Germany. I was still not happy nor did I feel like my life was going in the direction that God wanted for me. I cried constantly and tried to force situations to make things better. I was asking God for help but was still trying to do it on my own.

Prior to leaving for Germany we spent time visiting family and I can remember taking a family photo with my in-laws at the time and thinking I don't like any of this but it's what I chose so this is my life and I will just have to deal with it. I was letting go. I stopped crying and stopped trying to change things. I prayed and let God know that I knew I messed up and I was willing to suffer the consequences of my decisions. I continued to read the Bible and was determined to be the best Christian I could be.

Following our visit with family my first husband went to Germany and I went to live with my sister, Valerie, until he sent the required military orders for me to join him. About 6 weeks later he decided he no longer wanted to be married to me and that he would not send orders for me to join him overseas. All of my earthly belongings except the clothes I had packed in a small suitcase had already been shipped to Germany but I would not be accompanying them. I was devastated. I didn't have a job, I had very few clothes and I did not have a home.

After almost breaking under the initial heartache and pain I gained strength from the scriptures I read and realized that I had to totally rely on God.

I fully committed my heart and life to Jesus, accepting Him as my husband. Although I was homeless and had to rely on family to have a roof over my head I continued to trust and believe that God would turn things around and bring me to a better state. I began to learn more about Him and His ways and was determined to live the way He designed. The foundation of my life was now being formed properly and God was able to build a better life for me. I was able to reenlist in the Air Force which was a miracle from God; more on this later.

As you can see from my personal story trying to do it on your own is a recipe for disaster. Recognizing the need for God and allowing Him to be the architect allows the foundation to be built properly and it allows the building of your life to be formed correctly.

Know that even when you decide to allow God to be the architect you may still have things that need to be dug out of your life in order for the foundation to be built properly. I went through many emotionally and physically difficult days as the excess soil in my life was being removed. By continuing in the word of God and following the specific instructions Jesus has given it allowed, and continues to allow, God room to work. The next chapter goes into greater detail on excavation and having the proper soil.

◈THREE◈

How to Govern Oneself – Excavation

Keeping our stability through difficult days has more to do with developing our own character than what is actually happening around us. In our building example the soil needs to be removed below the frost line and above the water table. If it is not within this balanced state the foundation will experience damage. If we develop the character that Jesus requires of us we will be able to face any situation and not be moved. We will be balanced.

In the book of Matthew Jesus teaches us the character traits of being meek, allowing persecution, having a reputation of good works, honoring vows, not making oaths and trusting God.

Be Meek

> *Blessed are the meek: for they shall inherit the earth.* Matthew 5:5

Strong's Exhaustive Concordance of the Bible, the standard reference guide to those seeking a deeper meaning in the scriptures, defines the word meek in this passage as gentle and humble.[2]

---

[2] Strong, James. "Meek." *Strong's Expanded Exhaustive Concordance of the Bible*. Nashville: Thomas Nelson, 2009. Print.

Meek is also defined as teachable, not just the ability to learn but also the willingness to be taught even when you already have knowledge of a particular subject. It is also being patient under suffering as in this definition from Wikipedia:

> **Meekness** is a possible attribute of human nature and behavior. It has been defined several ways: righteous, humble, teachable, and patient under suffering willing to follow gospel teachings; an attribute of a true disciple.
> Meekness has been contrasted with humility as referring to behavior towards others, where humbleness refers to an attitude towards oneself - meekness meaning restraining one's own power, so as to allow room for others.[3]

Being meek is not being weak; it is being humble and esteeming others better than yourself see *Philippians 2:3.*

For my personal life example I will use the definition of restraining one's own power, so as to allow room for others. This vivid example of meekness that I experienced was during a time when I witnessed an encounter between a Pastor and a member of his congregation. I was living in Albuquerque, New Mexico and had the

---

[3] *Wikipedia contributors. "Meekness." Wikipedia, The Free Encyclopedia. Wikipedia, The Free Encyclopedia, 2 Sep. 2014. Web. 5 Sep. 2014.*

opportunity to serve as the office secretary of our church for a couple of years.

On this particular day I was finishing up some work in the office while waiting for my husband to come and take me to get a bite to eat before returning for our evening service. The office door swung open and the gentleman that was handling our computer security bolted in and loudly expressed his displeasure with the way Pastor desired to handle the computer security.

The next thing I know this young man was shouting and speaking very harshly to Pastor so much so that I wanted to rise up and fight back; how dare he speak to Pastor that way? But I looked at my pastor and he had a loving look on his face, he never got angry and he never spoke back in the way in which he was being spoken to. He was displaying the most perfect example of humility; he was acting like Jesus! My emotions were still raging inside of me but Pastor was calm and collected and loving. He spoke words that, if the young man would have received them, would bring restoration to this young man's heart and not make him feel any worse for his inappropriate actions. Every time I think of humility and what it means to be humble I think of this encounter.

In later years I learned the principle behind what this Pastor was doing. My current Pastor passed along teaching from his headship, Bishop Wellington Boone, who teaches us to be worms and not snakes. A snake will attack and bite when confronted but a worm has no defense mechanisms; it can never strike back.

Many people don't like worms, but I like them because I like planting flowers and when you add earthworms to a flower pot they improve the soil by burrowing and forming channels that the roots can grow down into and reach moisture. The worms also provide secretions that help the soil's ph level; keeping it from being too acidic or too alkalized over time. When we show humility and become worms we cultivate an atmosphere that allows those around us to draw from living water and we help keep the peace in a situation much like the earthworm does for soil.

Excavate your land properly and maintain the proper soil. Be meek, be humble; be a worm.

Allow Persecution

Noah Webster's 1928 dictionary of the English language defines persecution as, "the act or practice of persecuting; the infliction of pain, punishment or death upon others unjustly, particularly for adhering to a religious creed or mode of worship, either by way of penalty or for compelling them to renounce their principles." Thankfully I've never experienced a severe form of persecution as described in this definition so I cannot begin to share with you what it is truly like to experience punishment or death. I do acknowledge the sacrifice that so many Christians have endured in defense of the faith. However, I have experienced the emotional pain of not fitting in or not being accepted by the popular crowds because of standing up for my beliefs. I always think there is nothing that man can do to me that even begins to compare with what I would have to face if I chose not to serve God or if I renounced my beliefs. And by comparison, there is nothing that man can give me that is more desirable than what God has for me.

Look at how Jesus stood when He we being spat upon and ridiculed. His actions were prophesied about in the book of Isaiah and the fulfillment is recorded in the book of Matthew.

He was oppressed, and he was afflicted, yet he opened not his mouth: he is brought as a lamb to the slaughter, and as a sheep before her shearers is dumb, so he openeth not his mouth. Isaiah 53:8

[12] And when he was accused of the chief priests and elders, he answered nothing.[13] Then said Pilate unto him, Hearest thou not how many things they witness against thee? [14] And he answered him to never a word; insomuch that the governor marvelled greatly. Matthew 27:12-14

Jesus never said a word; He took the persecution without fighting back. This is the character that Jesus wants us to portray. Ask the Holy Spirit to help you become a person who won't fight back.

Have a Reputation of Good Works

When people think about others they usually know who can be trusted and who cannot be trusted. This knowing is based on past experiences of how the person handled themselves in various situations. When you trust someone to keep a secret and later find that your trust has been betrayed you know not to share secrets with that person. On the flip side when you share your heart with someone and they guard and protect you that person becomes a person you can trust. You often brag about them and tell others that they can be trusted, that person has a reputation of good works.

I do what I can to make sure I don't betray anyone's trust. If someone shares something with me I put it in what I call "The Vault." I don't talk about it with anyone, not even the person who told me unless they bring it up.

However, it does not stop there. How you respond in life's situations also builds the reputation that you have. God gave us examples of how to show a reputation of good works. Let's go to the Bible and look at one of those examples; the story of a person with a good reputation.

> *[1]In the third year of the reign of Jehoiakim king of Judah came Nebuchadnezzar king of Babylon unto Jerusalem, and besieged it. [2]And the Lord gave Jehoiakim king of Judah into his hand, with part of the vessels of the house of God: which he carried into the land of Shinar to the house of his god;*

and he brought the vessels into the treasure house of his god. ³And the king spake unto Ashpenaz the master of his eunuchs, that he should bring certain of the children of Israel, and of the king's seed, and of the princes; ⁴Children in whom was no blemish, but well favoured, and skilful in all wisdom, and cunning in knowledge, and understanding science, and such as had ability in them to stand in the king's palace, and whom they might teach the learning and the tongue of the Chaldeans. ⁵And the king appointed them a daily provision of the king's meat, and of the wine which he drank: so nourishing them three years, that at the end thereof they might stand before the king. ⁶Now among these were of the children of Judah, Daniel, Hananiah, Mishael, and Azariah: ⁷Unto whom the prince of the eunuchs gave names: for he gave unto Daniel the name of Belteshazzar; and to Hananiah, of Shadrach; and to Mishael, of Meshach; and to Azariah, of Abednego. ⁸But Daniel purposed in his heart that he would not defile himself with the portion of the king's meat, nor with the wine which he drank: therefore he requested of the prince of the eunuchs that he might not defile himself.⁹Now God had brought Daniel into favour and tender love with the prince of the eunuchs.¹⁰And the prince of the eunuchs said unto Daniel, I fear my lord the king, who hath appointed your meat and your drink: for why should he see your faces worse liking than the children which are of your sort? then shall ye make me endanger my head to the king.[11]Then said Daniel to Melzar, whom the prince of the eunuchs had set over Daniel, Hananiah, Mishael, and Azariah,[12]Prove thy servants, I beseech thee, ten days; and let them give us pulse to eat, and water to drink. [13]Then let our countenances be looked upon before thee, and the countenance of the children that eat of the portion of the king's meat: and as thou seest, deal with thy servants. [14]So he consented to them in this matter, and proved them ten days. [15]And at the end of ten days their countenances appeared fairer and fatter in flesh than all the children which did eat the portion of the king's meat. [16]Thus Melzar took away the portion of their meat, and the wine that they should drink; and gave them pulse. [17]As for these four children, God gave them knowledge and skill in all learning and wisdom: and Daniel had understanding in all visions and dreams. [18]Now at the end of the days that the king had said he should bring them in, then the prince of the eunuchs brought them in before Nebuchadnezzar. [19]And the king communed with them; and among them all was found none like Daniel, Hananiah, Mishael, and Azariah: therefore stood they before the king. [20]And in all matters of wisdom and understanding, that the king enquired of them, he found them ten times better than all the magicians and astrologers that were *in all his realm. ²¹And Daniel continued even unto the first year of king Cyrus.* Daniel 1:1-21

Daniel is a shining example of someone who proved himself to have a reputation of good works. God has given us this example to show us how to stand by the principles of God with humility and grace and be accepted of those who may not share our beliefs. God gave gifts to Daniel because He knew He could trust him to be a great representation of His kingdom.

We should always strive to do what is right and not give others truthful ammunition to speak bad things about us. If someone speaks badly about us falsely we can trust God to protect and vindicate us as He did in our example of Daniel. Continue reading the book of Daniel to see how God took care of him.

Honor Your Vows

The best way to honor your vows is to not make any. But there are several vows that we make regularly without thinking about them and many people break these vows without concern of eternal judgment. Any time you sign your name to a document you are making a vow; a vow that the information you have just given is correct, a vow that you will pay monies owed or a vow that you have read and understand the terms and conditions of a document.

Each one of these examples of vows should be taken seriously but so many of them have become commonplace that we don't think about the consequences. How many times have you signed a contract without first reading it? How can you know if you are breaking your vow if you don't know that to which you have agreed to? Become a person of integrity and do what you say you will do.

Don't Make Oaths

> Again, ye have heard that it hath been said by them of old time, Thou shalt not forswear thyself, but shalt perform unto the Lord thine oaths: [34] But I say unto you, Swear not at all; neither by heaven; for it is God's throne: [35] Nor by the earth; for it is his footstool: neither by Jerusalem; for it is the city of the great King. [36] Neither shalt thou swear by thy head, because thou canst not make one hair white or black. [37] But let your communication be, Yea, yea; Nay, nay: for whatsoever is more than these cometh of evil.
> Matthew 5:33-37

When you make oaths you find yourself obligated to that oath even if you cannot fulfill it. We don't know what the future holds, that is why I believe Jesus does not want us to make oaths at all. So what is an oath? Noah Webster describes it as:

A solemn affirmation or declaration, made with an appeal to God for the truth of what is affirmed. The appeal to God in an oath, implies that the person imprecates his vengeance and renounces his favor if the declaration is false, or if the declaration is a promise, the person invokes the vengeance of God if he should fail to fulfill it. A false oath is called perjury.[4]

Why would anyone make a promise that would possibly invoke the vengeance of God not knowing what the future holds? It just makes sense not to make oaths and thereby keep your building from toppling to the ground.

I like verse 37; it is basically saying if you mean yes say yes and if no say "no!" I've struggled with saying "no!" most of my life. However I find it is much easier to just say "no!" than to wiggle out of a situation later or find myself pulling my hair out because I've over-committed.

Stand strong on the word of God and trust the Holy Spirit to work each situation out with a Kingdom outcome. I find when I truly say what I mean with a gentleness of spirit, as the Bible directs, my words are well received and my life remains peaceful.

---

[4] Webster, Noah. "American Dictionary of the English Language." *Websters Dictionary 1828*. N.p., 1 Jan. 1828. Web. 23 June 2014. <http://webstersdictionary1828.com/>.

Trust God

Jesus tells us to trust God but often we find ourselves trusting in everything but God. We put our trust in money, jobs, our government – well maybe not so much, and even ourselves. It amazes me how God takes care of birds. My home office has windows that allow me to look out into our back yard while I'm working. I'm blessed daily by a variety of birds that find sanctuary within our fenced property.

God provides these birds with food and shelter. I watch them as they sing joyfully and play in our yard. I sometimes feel guilty because I seldom remember to hang or fill my bird feeders but they aren't suffering because of my neglect; God is taking care of them.

> *Behold the fowls of the air: for they sow not, neither do they reap, nor gather into barns; yet your heavenly Father feedeth them. Are ye not much better than they?* Matthew 6:26

Stephen and I have had many opportunities to trust God but none as daring as our cross-country move. We were led by God to leave Albuquerque, NM, to move closer to my sisters in North Carolina. We did not know where we would be living nor did we have jobs. But we knew God was leading us in this move and we desired to follow His leading and trust that He would take care of us.

We were told by our neighbors in Albuquerque that the real estate market was slow and homes in our neighborhood were not selling. Despite the naysayers our home sold for almost full asking price in less than one month. We trusted God.

Additionally when we arrived in North Carolina we both obtained permanent jobs in less than two weeks only to learn after we were employed that the local job market was a difficult one. Many newcomers could only find temporary or contract positions. Trusting God for us took on an even deeper meaning after learning that information.

The Bible is full of scriptures that instruct us to trust God, but the premise is that we acknowledge Him and put Him first in our lives. In the Bible, David writes in Psalm 37:25:

I have been young, and now am old; yet have I not seen the righteous forsaken, nor his seed begging bread.

The entire chapter of Psalm 37 gives encouragement to trust in, delight in, and commit your ways to the Lord. Notice David writes that he's never seen the righteous forsaken. You can only obtain righteousness through faith and trust in God. See Romans 4:3 and Hebrews chapter 11. Read and study these scripture passages to build your trust in God and help excavate the soil prior to continuing to build your foundation which continues with how we treat others.

❧FOUR❧

How Jesus Wants Us to Treat Others – Footings

Footings help spread the weight of the building and sometimes additional footings are added inside the structure to support load-bearing walls and prevent settling. Our footings or pathways help us build the support we need from others to keep our foundation from being crushed by pressure. One of my favorite sayings is "Many hands make light work." But we won't have those hands if we don't treat others they way Jesus instructs. He tells us to have compassion, to show mercy, to keep peace, and don't lust.

Have Compassion

The Holy Ghost has given me many lessons on having compassion. Some of these teachings are not what you may think as your typical example of seeing someone less fortunate and giving them your last ten dollars or even showing concern when someone is hurting. No the lessons I've had are on a much less visible level.

One lesson involved cleaning bathrooms. Yep! I learned to have compassion by cleaning bathrooms. At one time in my life I would go into a public bathroom and see the mess that was left by others and audibly fuss and complain and loudly ask why would anyone leave a place in such a mess.

You see my mother taught me to always pick up after myself and to leave a place better than I found it. I thought this was something everyone learned and if they are not following this rule then they are nasty slobs. I know that sounds harsh but you can see that I needed help from the Holy Ghost.

One day when I was going through this rant in yet another public bathroom the Holy Ghost told me to clean up the mess and leave it nice for the next person. What? Why should I clean up behind someone else? But thankfully I had gotten to a place in my life where I did what the Holy Ghost told me even though I did not want to. From that day on I found myself cleaning up every public bathroom I entered. I'm not talking about scrubbing toilets; I'm talking about picking up trash, toilet paper and toilet seat liners that are on the floor, putting them in the trash, flushing toilets left un-flushed and also wiping off the counter and making it look tidy for the next person.

I kept doing this until one day I asked the Holy Ghost, "How long do I have to clean up bathrooms. When can I just go to the bathroom and leave it alone?" The answer I received was, "Until you no longer have anger in your heart for those that left it a mess." This statement broke me. I finally got it. I needed to look at the people who trashed the toilets with the same love and compassion that God looks at us as we trash this world He lovingly created. I had to look beyond the fault and see the person. Not everyone is taught to clean up after themselves. Not everyone cares about leaving a place in better condition than when they arrive to it. I had to learn to show compassion and this was one way the Holy Spirit was teaching me. Being compassionate through our own eyes is often difficult. But having compassion through the eyes of Jesus is, and should always be, our goal. God forgave us, therefore we should forgive others.

And be ye kind one to another, tenderhearted, forgiving one another, even as God for Christ's sake hath forgiven you. Ephesians 4:32

Show Mercy

Blessed [are] the merciful: for they shall obtain mercy. Matthew 5:7

Mercy is not giving someone something they deserve. How many times have we relished in the fact that someone is getting what they deserve? They have done something wrong, most likely to ourselves and then we see them reaping the harvest of what they have sown (scripture) and we enjoy every minute of it. When we think this way, with a sense of satisfaction, we can understand what a great gift it is to give mercy.

Mercy does not come easy but when we decide to be merciful it puts us right in line with the character of Jesus. He is our ultimate example on being merciful.

Then said Jesus, Father, forgive them; for they know not what they do. And they parted his raiment, and cast lots. Luke 23:34

When you show mercy to others you acknowledge the mercy that God has given to you.

Keep Peace

Blessed [are] the peacemakers: for they shall be called the children of God. Matthew 5:9

I've had many opportunities to put the Christian virtue of peace into practice and the one experience that sticks out as an example I hope you can learn from is about a time when I was in the military. I was assigned a very large project that took several weeks to complete. Toward the end of the project, seeing all the work that was required, my commander assigned another Non-Commissioned Officer to assist me. This newly-assigned assistant rarely made herself available to me and I completed the project on my own.

However, when it came time to present the completed project she pushed her way forward and boldly took all the credit; never acknowledging the work I had done. It was in front of several high ranking officials. She was applauded and recognized for the great work that was done.

I could have stepped up, created a scene and embarrassed her, myself and our commander but miraculously I never said a word, I kept the peace. I say miraculously because it is not something that I would have normally done. Although it hurt deeply that someone else got the credit for the work I had done I never brought it up to my superiors.

How was I able to react this way? My answer is that after I got off work each day I would spend countless hours reading my Bible. I had recently rededicated my life to God and all I wanted to do was to read the Bible for myself. I did not know or understand what it was doing for me but I continued to read because I was amazed at how lively and interesting it was. It wasn't until years later that I learned this principle was called engrafting the word into your heart. Jesus talks about this principle in the gospel of Mark.

> [26] He also said, "This is what the kingdom of God is like. A man scatters seed on the ground. [27] Night and day, whether he sleeps or gets up, the seed sprouts and grows, though he does not know how. [28] All by itself the soil produces grain—first the stalk, then the head, then the full kernel in the head. [29] As soon as the grain is ripe, he puts the sickle to it, because the harvest has come." Mark 4:26-29

By reading the word and planting it into my heart I was able to keep the peace and allow someone else to take the credit. Developing the character of Jesus involves spending time in the word of God and letting it become a part of you.

Don't Lust

Lust is a word that is often used in sexual connotations, however the definition of lust is broader in its description;

> **LUST,** *noun*
> **1.** Longing desire; eagerness to possess or enjoy; as the *lust* of gain.
> My *lust* shall be satisfied upon them. Exodus 15:9.
> **2.** Concupiscence; carnal appetite; unlawful desire of carnal pleasure. Romans 1:27. 2 Peter 2:10.
> **3.** Evil propensity; depraved affections and desires. James 1:14. Psalms 81:12.[5]

From this definition you can see that lust is much more than sexual desire. Jesus telling us not to lust carries with it not desiring anything that would take us into a carnal or evil mindset. He warns us not to desire what others have. Lust will surely cause our foundation to be weak as lust is used twice when describing all that is in the world; *"Lust of the eyes, Lust of the flesh and the pride of life."* 1 John 2:16.

An effective way to keep from falling into the trap of lust for things is to learn to be thankful to God for what you have and trust that He will increase you in His own timing. According to U.S. standards for living I've lived at the

---

[5] Webster, Noah. "American Dictionary of the English Language." *Websters Dictionary 1828.* N.p., 1 Jan. 1828. Web. 26 May 2014. <http://webstersdictionary1828.com/>.

poverty level or dangerously close to the poverty level many times in my life. But I never wanted for anything because God always provided. Don't get me wrong, I love having nice, quality things, but I'm content with what I have until God provides better. This contentment makes it so much easier to appreciate what others may have and to not lust after their things. Maintaining this attitude helps in our next step in building our foundation which is how Jesus wants us to relate toward God.

❧FIVE❧

How Jesus Wants us to Relate Toward God – Foundation Walls

The walls of our building hold the building up and serve as the frame work for the structure. How we relate toward God is the framework of our being.

In our building example the foundation walls are poured between sets of form work that is not to be removed until the concrete gains full strength. I like to think the form work in our lives is a vibrant Bible believing body of believers, a local church that helps us gain strength.

To build our foundation walls Jesus tells us that there is only one way to God, to serve only God, to store treasures in heaven and to trust God.

One Way to God

I have a saying on my desk that I found in the early 1980's, that reads "What is popular Is not always right and what is right is not always popular." I don't know who wrote this quote but it has served me well through the years as a reminder that following the crowd may not be the best thing to do.

Jesus tells us to enter in the straight (narrow, from obstacles standing close about) gate (entrance). The entrance to God is only by way of Jesus where as the gate to hell is broad; there are many ways to get in.

If you pay attention to what humans say you will find that there are many who believe there are several paths that lead to God. However Jesus very plainly tells us there is only one way. I choose to believe Jesus and not man. Jesus even rebuked Peter and called him Satan when he had his mind set on the things of man.

> But he turned and said to Peter, "Get behind me, Satan! You are a hindrance to me. For you are not setting your mind on the things of God, but on the things of man." Matthew 16:23

A true study of God's word will reveal God's plan of salvation through Jesus Christ. I know I am being very straight forward here but the bottom line is either you believe it or you don't.

Be Single Minded and Serve Only God.

This is the first commandment handed down to the children of Israel from Moses. Single mindedness means that you have one aim, one purpose.

There are many avenues in life and there are many counselors that will help you determine which path to take. They tell you to focus on what you like to do and give surveys to complete to find your interests. There isn't anything wrong with seeking out your interests and passions and choosing a particular path in life. However, in all of your seeking your primary goal should be to serve God. Whatever occupation you choose, it should ultimately be to serve God.

Many people choose an occupation for the sole reason that it will pay them well. Trust God to take care of you. Seek Him first and don't worry about tomorrow.

The messages of our current society don't allow for a single-minded approach toward God, but we must strive to reach this goal if we are to have a stable foundation. James 1:8 tells us that a double minded man is unstable in all his ways.

Store Your Treasure in Heaven

God has many great things in store for us, which is why He tells us don't store treasure on earth, let our treasure be in heaven.

So what is treasure? It is what you value. You've heard the saying, "one man's trash is another man's treasure." What makes the difference is the value you place on it. If you value a car, that car becomes your focus. You protect it by parking it away from other cars to make sure you don't get dings on it and you may even get a cover for it so it isn't damaged by the elements. You spend time talking about it and may even have a special name for it. But a car is basically a means of transportation; it has no eternal value and will deteriorate and decay.

19 Lay not up for yourselves treasures upon earth, where moth and rust doth corrupt, and where thieves break through and steal: 20 But lay up for yourselves treasures in heaven, where neither moth nor rust doth corrupt, and where thieves do not break through nor steal: 21 For where your treasure is, there will your heart be also. Matthew 6:19-21

The question is, "What are the treasures that cannot be corrupted or stolen?" God has given us His love through Christ Jesus; this is a free gift that cannot be stolen away. Another thing that cannot be taken is the word of God that we hide in our hearts. Psalms 119:11 says, *"Thy word have I hid in my heart that I might not sin against thee."*

Again, Trust God

I covered this topic earlier in chapter 3; however it cannot be expressed enough. Mark 11:22 tells us to have faith in God. When we trust God the outcome of our circumstances is far better than what we could come up with on our own. God has more wisdom, more insight and more resources than we could ever imagine.

When I was in transition from my first marriage I didn't have a home, very little clothing and no vision for the future. Little did I know God had set a plan in motion before I even knew I would be in this storm of life.

Several months earlier I had the opportunity to meet an individual who was on temporary duty in Louisiana at

Barksdale Air Force Base where I was stationed. This person sang, played the piano and joined with our gospel choir while he was there. Our group enjoyed him and we spent a few long nights singing and praising God together during his short stay.

Fast forward about 6 months to Rochester, NY where I was living with my sister while awaiting spousal accompaniment orders from my husband so that I could join him in Germany. This is where I learned that I would not be accompanying him and that he no longer desired to be married to me.

I had no source of income so I took a temporary job and contemplated what my future would be. The singer/pianist that I met months earlier just so happened to be an Air Force recruiter stationed in Rochester, NY. I made contact with him and had dinner with his wife and family. Being a Christian couple they asked how I was doing and if there was something they could pray with me about. I opened up to them about my current status and he asked me if I had considered returning to the Air Force.

I told him that I had thought about this briefly but unfortunately when I left I signed a document saying that I was aware that I would not be able to reenlist in the Air Force. He was familiar with the regulations surrounding this requirement but thought that there may be legislation that had recently been introduced that canceled out the letter I signed.

Seven months later I reenlisted in the Air Force and was on my way to my new duty station in Hampton, VA. Throughout the year and three months that I was out of the Air Force and awaiting the new chapter of my life to begin, I chose to put my trust in God. I could have forced my way into several options but God's plan proved to be the most beneficial for me. After signing the letter that I could not return to the Air Force, I eventually retired from the Air Force after 21 years of service. And it was in Hampton, VA that I met and married my current husband of 26 years (as of the writing of this book). By trusting God my outcome was far better than I could imagine for myself.

The life of Joseph gives us a clear Biblical example of putting your complete trust in God. I encourage you to read his story in Genesis chapters 37 through 50. Even if you have already read this account go back and read it again. Each time I read it I gain new insight and strength that enables me to put my trust in God.

Conclusion

> *"Therefore whosoever heareth these sayings of mine, and doeth them, I will liken him unto a wise man, which built his house upon a rock:* [25] *And the rain descended, and the floods came, and the winds blew, and beat upon that house; and it fell not: for it was founded upon a rock.* [26] *And every one that heareth these sayings of mine, and doeth them not, shall be likened unto a foolish man, which built his house upon the sand:* [27] *And the rain descended, and the floods came, and the winds blew, and beat upon that house; and it fell: and great was the fall of it."* Matthew 7:24-27

With a sure foundation you will be able to withstand the storms that are going to come, you may have to bend and undulate much like the temporary housing building I was in while stationed in Guam however just like that building a sure foundation will keep you from sustaining major damage. At the end of the storm you will find yourself still standing.

Keep your focus on the word of God. A visiting evangelist once gave me a visual that helps remind me of this. She called people out from the congregation who needed prayer. I was in the midst of separation from my first husband and was pretty much an emotional wreck experiencing this storm. She told me to take my Bible and put it on the floor. I thought it was strange but obeyed out of curiosity. She then told me to place both feet squarely on the Bible and simply said, "Stand on the word of God!" This exercise may have seemed basic and unimpressive, however, I believe the Holy Spirit took it and made something happen inside my heart. I was no longer reeling with emotion but able to stand with a new confidence that everything would be alright. I began reading and studying the Bible like I never had before.

The principles that Jesus gave us are difficult at times for our souls to grab hold to and walk out in our daily lives. That is why we need the Holy Spirit of God to help us and impart the supernatural strength we need. We can only gain this through standing on the word, reading and meditating on it and making it a priority in our lives.

Excavate your land properly and maintain the proper soil. Be humble; be a worm.

When we die to our own agenda and give ourselves over to the leading of the Holy Spirit by the word of God we build a foundation that is sure.

It is my sincere hope that this book has led you to dig deeper into the scriptures and develop a relationship with God that is above all other relationships in your life. We all have life problems, issues, challenges, interruptions or whatever you want to call them. Reading the Bible and learning more about the character of God and how to handle these things will make your foundation sure and your building will stand. An excellent book to read to bring a Godly perspective to life's challenges is Ecclesiastes. I especially like the last two verses:

> [13]Now all has been heard; here is the conclusion of the matter: Fear God and keep his commandments, for this is the duty of all mankind. [14] For God will bring every deed into judgment, including every hidden thing, whether it is good or evil. Ecclesiastes 12:13-14

In all of the writer's wisdom he concludes that we should fear God and keep his commandments. Be diligent in building and maintaining your walls; Ecclesiastes 10:18 cautions us that slothfulness causes the building to decay.

But what if we haven't kept His commandments, what if we have already fallen short and messed things up by starting off with the wrong preparation for our building? Thankfully God in His love, grace and mercy has given us a way to make things right

> My little children, these things write I unto you, that ye sin not. And if any man sin, we have an advocate with the Father, Jesus Christ the righteous: [2]And he is the propitiation for our sins: and not for ours only, but also for the sins of the whole world. [3]And hereby we do know that we know him, if we keep his commandments. [4]He that saith, I know him, and keepeth not his commandments, is a liar, and the truth is not in him. [5]But whoso keepeth his word, in him verily is

the love of God perfected: hereby know we that we are in him. 1 John 2:1-5

I end with the words of Jesus;

I encourage you to continue daily in the word of God, build a sure foundation so you will be perfect-complete-in various applications of labor, growth, mental and moral character. Matthew 5:48

www.ingramcontent.com/pod-product-compliance
Lightning Source LLC
Chambersburg PA
CBHW071025040426
42443CB00007B/933